Jack C.

The Awakening

Poems
Newly Found

Jack Clemo

The Awakening

Poems Newly Found

Edited by John Hurst, Alan M. Kent
and Andrew C. Symons

Francis
Boutle
Publishers

First published by Francis Boutle Publishers
272 Alexandra Park Road
London N22 7BG
Tel/Fax: 020 8889 7744
Email: clemo@francisboutle.demon.co.uk
www.francisboutle.demon.co.uk

ISBN 1903427 17 7

Printed in Spain

Contents

Acknowledgements

The editors would like to thank the following people for their comments and assistance in the assembly of this volume: Ruth Clemo, Bella Peaty, Father Benedict Ramsden, Lilah Ramsden, Charles Thomas, John C.C. Probert, Helen Blake, Paul Annear, Michael Spinks, James Whetter, Charles Thurlow, Tim Saunders, the Lockwood Memorial Library, Buffalo University, USA and the staff of Wheal Martyn Museum, St Austell, especially Dr Brian Strathen. We would like to thank the University of Exeter Library (Special Collection), the owners of the Jack Clemo papers (EUL MS 68), for their permission to publish these poems, in particular Dr Jessica Gardner for her efforts. And we would like to thank Macmillan, London, UK for permission to reprint in the introduction Charles Causley's 'Homage to Jack Clemo' from *Collected Poems 1951–1975*.

Introduction

Jack Clemo: A Life

On 11 March, 1916, Jack Clemo was born in clay-miner's cottage at Goonamarris, near St Stephen-in-Brannel in mid Cornwall. The joy of the event for his parents, Evelyn and Reggie Clemo, was quickly overshadowed by the horrors of war. Reggie was aboard the destroyer H.M.S. Tornado on 23 December, 1917, when she was mined and lost with all hands. Evelyn, surviving on a war-widow's pension, came close to breakdown three years later. One morning at breakfast, she noticed a film covering Jack's right eye. 'A moment of prophetic revelation', given to her through a passage from Isaiah, as she explains in her autobiography *I Proved Thee at the Waters* (1976), provided the foundation for the rest of her life.[1] Even as late as 1987, Jack Clemo remained convinced of the importance of the event:

We can no longer find stability in any church. That's why I've stressed the individual experience, the 'personal covenant with God'. When you've had an amazing answer to prayer, or an overwhelming proof of divine guidance through a Bible text, you are no longer worried about church 'authority' or the lack of it! My mother's life and mine were based on her Isaiah 'promise': 'Thy children shall be taught of the Lord'... it has been literally fulfilled ...[2]

Paradoxically, Clemo's residual sightedness and growing maturity led him from the age of fourteen to reject Christianity. On 27 April, 1929, while attending a wedding reception at Penrose Veor farm, below St Dennis Carne, he was overwhelmed with romantic passion for a local girl called Evelyn Phillips and the sense of a pantheistic power in nature.[3] From that moment on he spurned organised religion and any conventional mode of life. Poetry and the erotic became the impulse of his existence. At a more mundane level he earned a meagre living writing Cornu-English dialect stories for almanacs and newspapers.[4] Eight years were to pass before rejection and disillusionment caused him to ponder again his sensual quest.

Interestingly, Penrose Farm, mentioned in *Confession of a Rebel* (1949) over a dozen times, and the whole area from which Clemo drew his inspiration at this period are redolent of legend. In addition to the Arthurian associations to the north, the Fowey and Fal estuaries to the south are steeped in Tristan and Iseult place-names.[5] How these associations, centred on themes of passionate and erotic love, influenced Clemo is a matter for speculation, yet we sense an affinity and continuity.

During the 1940s Clemo appears to have destroyed or reworked much of what he wrote. The present collection, with poems dating from 1934, is both important and problematic. In 1937–8, a series of mystical experiences of varying degrees of intensity, received while walking the industrial china clay country of the St Stephen-in-Brannel district, brought Clemo back to the Christian religion but not to the Church. He interpreted these experiences as encounters with a divine person, the 'risen Christ' of Christian theology. This can be seen from such poems as 'Towards the Dawn' (undated), 'Warmth' (dated 7/8/37) and the later 'Christ in the Clay-pit' (written 1945, published 1947). Some of the poems of the 1937–1950 period show direct visionary inspiration. Others appear more contrived, while a third group have form as the dominant consideration. A last group suggest a reworking of poems from the Penrose Veor period, in the light of the clayscape Christ-mysticism. Put more theologically, it is the re-assessment of natural religion from the perspective of revealed or supernatural religion.

An example of this is 'Revelation in the Clay Pit' (dated 12/5/46). It is a draft or variation of 'Prisoner of God', originally published in *The Clay Verge* (1951), and later included in *The Map of Clay* (1961). In a conversation in 1975 Clemo explained how the work of 'Prisoner of God' expressed his thwarted love for Evelyn Phillips, a relationship which foundered in 1934.[6] Evelyn then married and passed out of his life. The poet claimed it to have been the 'unhappiest poem I ever wrote', suggesting it originated in that fateful year. This would account for the emotional intensity of the opening lines. In 'Revelations in the Clay Pit' the directness is muted through use of the past tense:

> Who needs forgiveness now?
>   For You had poisoned me
> within the walls of pain-dark mystery
>   And left her free to vow
> Her life to other ends and so escape
> These damps you chose for me ...

If the 'had' is changed to 'have' and 'was' to 'is' later in line nine, which better fits the 'now' of line one, then it exactly describes the 1934 rejection of the poet by the girl. Clemo, therefore, appears to have taken a sketch from 1934–5, and reinterpreted it with a Christian resolution some years afterwards. The main body of work relating to the Christ-mysticism phase of the late 1930s and 1940s was published in three slim volumes, later united in *The Map of Clay*, with an introduction by Charles Causley.[7] *The Awakening* contains much of the rest.

While Clemo's poems were occasional pieces, he worked at novel writing tirelessly. The breakthrough, after a decade of rejections, came in 1947, when Chatto & Windus accepted *Wilding Graft*.[8] It won for him, in 1948, an Atlantic Award in Literature from Birmingham University. The only other novels to achieve publication had to wait another forty years. *The Shadowed Bed*, first drafted in 1938, was not published until 1986.[9] *The Clay Kiln*, came out in 2000, six years after the writer's death.[10] This last novel is particularly significant for its autobiographical detail, and needs to be read in conjunction with *Confessions of a Rebel*. Both relate to the poems of *The Awakening*.

It is all too apparent that the early 1950s saw a decline in the intensity of Clemo's mystical perceptions, with a concomitant diminution in creative activity. Then in 1955, disaster struck. Already partially deaf, he went completely blind. The last few months of fading sight were spent on a theological work called *The Invading Gospel* (1958). It represents a call for traditional Catholics and Protestants to resist the advances of theological modernism or liberal Protestantism.[11] At another level, it shows Clemo's religious development through contact with a range of

Protestant and Catholic writers. An exploration of the 'priest and lover' theme from Robert Browning was to have dramatic significance.[12] Clemo's polemic is the endeavour of a novelist rather than a theologian, with the telling phrase all too often displacing the dry, precise one. It is the last work to employ the problematic terms 'neo-' or 'modified Calvinist'. He used it to distance himself from the Calvinist fundamentalist position imposed upon him by J.C. Trewin and H.J. Wilmott in *London-Bodmin*.[13] By 1958, as the dust-jacket of *The Map of Clay* states, he had moved from a dogmatic Calvinism to a 'broader Evangelical faith'. Thereafter, he simply used the term 'Christian'.[14]

Severe disability, erotic frustration and spiritual aridity after 1955 saw Clemo descend into a 'dark night of the soul'. From these years came the poems found in *Cactus on Carmel* (1967).[15] The 'Carmel' of the title appears to allude to the 'dark night' described in the writings of the Spanish Carmelite, John of the Cross. John knew it as a time without spiritual or sensual consolation, where the soul cleaves to God in blind faith. The renunciation of Clemo's erotic-nature mysticism is evident in the poems 'Eros in Exile' and 'Carmel'. In 'Carmel' he contrasts the celibate spirituality of the French Carmelite, St Thérèse of Lisieux, with the New Testament wedding feast at Cana, interpreted as the union of sensual and spiritual. For Clemo, the possibility of release did not appear until 1967, when Ruth Peaty of Weymouth 'chanced' writing to him. From the time of his mother's 1937 Christmas present, *The Browning Love Letters*, he had conceived of marriage as a divine gift. The disability of Elizabeth Barrett proved no bar to Robert Browning's love. Clinging to the 'Browning pattern' (see 'Robert Browning'), Ruth and Jack were married on Saturday, 26 October, 1968 at Trethosa Chapel, with Charles Causley as best man. Marriage opened the second phase of mystical experience and creative activity, although centred on poetry rather than prose. It was no longer typified by intense visionary moments leading to relapse, as occurred between 1937 and 1950. Nor was it informed by the anger, resentment and depression evident in *The Map of Clay*. The 'dark night' had done its work. The mysticism of the new phase was more uninterrupted and mellow.

When Clemo saw *The Marriage of a Rebel* published in 1980,

twelve years of married life lay behind him. He concludes the book with the death of his mother on 3 June, 1977, and increasing contacts with Ruth's former home in Weymouth. Evelyn Clemo had retained to the end the revivalistic Methodism of her youth. She had disapproved of the Calvinistic influence on Jack's writing in the 1940s, and had borne the brunt of his disabilities in the 1950s.[16] The publication of *I Proved Thee at the Waters* in 1976 was, to her, the final vindication of her struggle and the 'promise' given in 1921. For Clemo *The Marriage of a Rebel* concluded a decade of intense creativity, including completion of two of this finest collections, *The Echoing Tip* (1971) and *Broad Autumn* (1975).[17] The autobiography is subtitled *A Mystical-erotic Quest*, a quest opening at Penrose Veor farm in 1929 and closing in erotic and creative fulfilment at the Clemo home in Goonamarris. As a closing curtain, in April, the BBC Everyman series screened a drama-documentary covering his early life under the title, 'A Different Drummer'.

The 1980s brought profound change to the lives of Jack and Ruth Clemo. The isolation of Goonamarris, the clay lorries passing at five in the morning and the failure of clayscape to function as a poetic vehicle, led them to move to Ruth's former home in Weymouth on 19 October, 1984:

This is the last time I shall write to you from the clay country. All is being arranged for our move to Weymouth ... Trethosa chapel members are giving us a farewell party tomorrow – a touching gesture to the 'prodigal son'. We leave Cornwall with goodwill and all wounds healed.

After eight months in Weymouth I have settled into the suburban routine and Cornwall has grown dim and remote ... *South-West Review* published poem I wrote on 'Leaving my Birthplace' and it will be reprinted in an anthology of *South-West Review* poems this autumn. It begins brusquely: "Don't talk of my being uprooted ..." I never feel that I've lost my roots: the immediate scene is only incidental if one functions from an inner faith.[18]

At Weymouth, Clemo made many new contacts, none more important than with Father Benedict and Lilah Ramsden. The Very Reverend Father Benedict Ramsden is Head of the Orthodox Community of St Anthony and St Elias in Totnes, Devon, which ministers to the severely mentally ill. Baffled in his search for the poet in Cornwall, he returned only to discover him in Weymouth. It proved a major step in Clemo's ecumenical contacts. During 1989 he made frequent references to Catholicism in his letters:

> The R.C. poet Elizabeth Jennings did a long review of *A Different Drummer* in Tablet three years ago, but the Catholic papers haven't noticed *Selected Poems*.
>
> I remain sympathetic to the Marian concepts, and was pleased recently when the BBC told me they may broadcast my poem 'Virgin Harbour'... I've written almost as many Catholic poems as explicitly Calvinist ones, and an article might be devoted exclusively to these – from 'Beyond Lourdes' to 'Wamba Convent'.[19]

However, the Marian theme was far from new. The present collection contains 'The Divine Lover', dated 16 December, 1938:

> Mid all the world's strange sorrow
> I know a strange relief:
> That God has kissed Our Lady
> And Their son has kissed our grief.

Clemo's understanding of erotic mysticism was finding support from a Catholic source. In 1975, the year *Broad Autumn* was published, Father Bede Griffiths, a Bendictine living in an Indian ashram on the River Cavery, was writing *Return to the Centre* (1976).[20] Father Bede argued in chapter eight, 'The Mystery of Love', how sexual union, when freed from the reductionist tendencies of Western secularism, opens man to the experience of transcendent and divine mystery. Unconsciously echoing 'The Divine Lover', Father Bede continues by saying that God's marriage to Mary – 'God has kissed Our Lady' – produced Jesus, the new man – 'Their son' – with human marriage as a symbol of this divine marriage, wherein the mystery of love finds fulfilment. In Clemo, the sense of human and divine marriage and its ultimate significance is nowhere clearer than in the late Italian-inspired works. Following his marriage to Ruth, Clemo believed himself to have emerged from the horrors of the 'dark night' to the peace and joy of mature belief. The Italian works show the final harmonising of the Protestant 'Browning pattern' with the 'mystical marriage' of Catholic spirituality. The two trips Jack and Ruth Clemo made to Italy, the first to Venice in October 1987 and the second to Florence and Venice in September 1993, were arranged by Father Benedict and Lilah Ramsden. In a letter dated 11 June, 1999, Father Benedict reflected:

I have always thought of Jack not only as a poet, as he thought of himself, a mystic ... When the idea of a trip to Venice cropped up in conversation, Jack's immediate excitement struck me, at the time, as much more than anticipation of a holiday. There was, of course, the immediate fact that this trip fitted his 'Browning pattern'. Venice had only come up because, while visiting Ca Rezzonico, I discovered that it was the place were Browning died and I sent Jack a postcard.[21]

More important than Ca Rezzonico was Casa Guidi in Florence. In a letter dated 18 November, Clemo wrote:

Benedict took us to Florence first, and we went to Casa Guidi palace, where the Brownings lived for 15 years. The place is empty and closed to the public, but we were admitted after Benedict showed the curator a copy of *Approach to Murano* and explained Browning's influence on me. I was deeply moved, standing in the study where he wrote 'Christmas Eve' and 'Easter Day'. Ruth and I were photographed on the balcony where Robert and Elizabeth so often paced up and down ... I've managed to write one or two poems about Florence, all positive about dreams coming true.[22]

His poem 'Palazzo Rezzonico' appears in *Approach to Murano* (1993), while the moving 'Casa Guidi' comes in *The Cured Arno* (1995).[23] Of all these Italian works, none surpasses the six stanzas of 'Late Honeymoon', with its romantic associations and Franciscan imagery. Unable to afford a honeymoon when first wed, Jack saw the visit to Venice as a belated gift to Ruth. In the intense use of rhyme, alliteration and assonance, 'Late Honeymoon' of c.1993 bears a remarkable similarity to 'Perranporth' of 1934.

The publication of *Approach to Murano* faced Clemo with the enduring hostility and incomprehension of the literary and religious establishments:

Few critics note my spiritual development – hence *The Times* lament over the lack of 'fierceness' in my later work. A Christian can't remain stuck at his starting point: he must expand with the fulfilment of God's promises.

The Cornish Banner is still the only Cornish paper which has reviewed *Murano*. Its anti-clay bias may upset people who like reading about 'Clemo's beloved clay-tips', but of course, I only reject the grim and desolate landscape as a symbol of my present life and faith.[24]

During this period, *The Cornish Banner* was Clemo's main support in Cornwall, publishing his poems and critical studies about his work.[25] Jack Clemo died on 24 July, 1994, in Weymouth. Of their last meeting, Father Benedict recorded in a letter of 11 June, 1999:

I remember my last meeting with him. As I left the hospital ward, I looked back and saw the ravaged man to whom I had just tried to convey the homage I felt. He was utterly transformed. He was lying on his pillow, his hands lifted towards his wife, his lips pursed to kiss hers. For a moment, all ravage fell away, and I was left with my last glimpse of him, as a lover. His marriage was, for him, a symbol of an even greater joy. I see that joy as something planned, constructed, organised, contrived even, but in now way do I doubt its transcendent significance.[26]

Andrew C. Symons

The Manuscripts
Clemo deposited the manuscripts of his work in the rare book room of the University of Exeter progressively from 1980 until his death in 1994. Subsequently, in 1992, a substantial quantity of manuscripts and memorabilia was placed in the Wheal Martyn China Clay Museum near St Austell. Although there is some overlap of material the two collections are somewhat different in character and complement each other usefully. The Exeter archive consists, for the most part, of detailed working papers and enables both the complex history of the novels to be traced and the evolution of almost all the major poetry. The Wheal Martyn collection has a more local focus, and contains valuable and interesting early correspondence, drafts of devotional papers, and a significant number of unpublished Cornu-English dialect stories

similar in style and character to those published in *The Bouncing Hills*. Both contain some poems clearly intended for publication, but which, for a variety of reasons remained unpublished. It seemed to us that the majority of these warranted publication, both for their intrinsic quality and for the light they throw on Clemo's development as a poet. It is clear in some cases that, on reflection, the poet did not want to publish certain poems and the editors have respected this wish. Clemo's manuscripts are notoriously difficult to decipher at times, so a few poems have not been included because it has been felt it would be impossible to establish an accurate text.

The most substantial single group of unpublished poems are to be found in the Exeter archive and were intended for publication in his first volume of poetry, *The Clay Verge*.[27] The reason for their exclusion is made clear in *The Marriage of a Rebel*:

For several months I had been building up the manuscript of *The Clay Verge* including all the violent anti-church and anti-nature poems which I had already outgrown. I tried to balance these by putting in revised versions of some of my quieter pre-war pieces; and also the more human and tender love poems ... The complete manuscript contained forty poems, but when I sent it to my publishers they used a dramatic blue pencil on it, weeding out twenty-three poems which they regarded as immature or redundant or not in keeping with the special flavour of the poems. They or – perhaps Day Lewis – evidently wished the aesthetic tone of the whole book to be harsh and sombre ... This troubled me because I felt the seventeen poems that remained did not give a true or fair picture of me or my beliefs as they were in 1950. Many of the excluded poems appeared in my later volumes.[28]

Although the greater part of Clemo's literary efforts during the 1930s had been directed to the writing of fiction, leading eventually to the publication in 1948 of *Wilding Graft*, and a few of the Cornu-English dialect stories had been published in such local magazines as *Doidge's Annual* and *Netherton's Almanack*, he came near to publication as a poet in 1934 when the publisher C.W. Daniel indicated willingness to publish the poetic sequence 'Twilight Where God Dwells' under a shared cost arrangement. It proved quite impossible in his then straitened circumstances for Clemo to proceed under this arrangement, and the full sequence remains unpublished to this day. Though it marks an important stage in Clemo's development as a writer and Daniel's agreement to be associated with its appearance indicated the degree of poetic merit that he must have discerned in it, in the long run its non-appearance has probably been of advantage to Clemo's reputation as a writer. It is a thinly dramatised version of his unhappy courtship of the girl Evelyn, recounted at some length in *Confession of a Rebel*, but although Clemo's verbal power and, to some extent, his control of verse forms are already present, the emotion is too raw, the experience inadequately distanced to constitute a genuine poetic achievement. Clemo made no further attempt to publish it, but several poems from the sequence are among those in the original contents of *The Clay Verge* and are, therefore, to be found in this collection, for example, 'Midnight of the Soul' and 'Good Friday'. There is a full manuscript of the sequence in the Exeter archive, and of part of the sequence in the Wheal Martyn collection. We have taken the decision to respect Clemo's intentions and only print those poems which, by inclusion in the planned contents of *The Clay Verge* he clearly wished to be preserved. Some may have seemed to make little sense outside their place in the sequence. In some cases Clemo may have felt that they were too unbalanced, and indeed indiscreet in as much as the identity of Evelyn was well known. His selection of poems for inclusion probably represents a balanced judgment regarding quality.

The poems do represent well the different strands of his poetic make-up. There is, for instance, the firm rooting in the clay-country into which he was born and in which he grew up. 'Goonamarris' evokes the precise area around the cottage he shared with his mother and her sister. The 'clay-splashed birthplace of my moods' solitudes' expresses forcefully the mixture of fascination and repulsion at the heart of his perception of the open-cast mining landscape, half-regretting the clay tips' assault on the rural environment, half welcoming its abrasive destruction of shallow notions of rural beauty. There is something of the 'pathetic fallacy' in the way in which even in these early poems he established a correlation between the isolation of its ravaged landscape and his own situation; and there is an element of melodramatic gesture in his conscious assertion of difference here and elsewhere in the collection.

Some of the poems with specific local reference (for example 'Snowfall at Kernick') were selected for inclusion in *The Clay Verge*, but 'Goonamarris' together with 'St Dennis' root this collection firmly and specifically in the locality where he was born and where he lived until 1984. As well as the poems retained from 'Twilight Where God Dwells' there are other indications of his attempts to establish his identity as a poet. 'Perranporth, August 15th, 1934' is an example of a type of poem which became common as his poetic career developed – inspired by one of the initially quite rare escapes from the claustrophobia of Goonamarris Slip – poems of holiday mood which allow a broadening of his perceptions of places and of the people associated with them, culminating in the fine poems of his last years relating to his two visits to Italy. 'The Legend of the Blackrock' on the other hand, marks an experiment that did not develop. Written very much in the style of Robert Stephen Hawker – the poet-parson of Morwenstow – and relating to a similar theme, it is an attractive and in its own terms successful essay in the ballad style. Clemo, clearly, did not feel however that this type of writing was central to his concerns and the attempt was not repeated. This is not to say that Clemo excluded light verse from his interests. There are several light pieces in *The Bouncing Hills* and a group of these arise from his gentle friendships with young girls. More considered poems evoking the unselfconscious femininity of his young friends from Goonamarris days are to be found in *The Clay Verge* (for example, 'The Plundered Fuschias' and 'The Child Traitor'). Not selected for inclusion there, so printed here are 'Clay Fairy' and 'The Token'. Both poems are clear in their assertion and evocation of the transforming nature of these friendships, and the use of religious terminology in them is calculated. The friendship of the girls is seen clearly as a means of grace. The story is clearly and directly told, without blurring the element of misunderstanding in the central chapters of *Confession of a Rebel*. Clemo makes clear his awareness of the manner in which this area of experience is both rare and intrinsically healthy. In defining his understanding he was much helped by his reading of the writer Theodore Francis Powys, especially his novel *Unclay* (1931) where he writes of a friendship between a middle-aged man and a girl of nine as a 'very beautiful and spiritually significant thing'.[29] It is this theological dimension in his understanding of this area of experience, which was powerful, rare, and distinctive.

The hallmark, indeed, of the majority of these poems is the power of their theological understanding and the linguistic vigour and firmly crafted verse in which that understanding is couched. Clemo himself freely acknowledges in *Confession of a Rebel* that his rendering of the basic doctrines of Puritan nonconformity are stated in a particularly rigorist form, doctrines which he comes to 'mature without discarding' in later years. Rooted in the language not only of the Bible but of Methodist hymnody ('Bringing in the Sheaves') and mediated through theological terminology (for example 'De Profundis') the poems give trenchant expression to doctrines that are both fully orthodox and yet highly individual and distinctive in the perspective from which they are presented. 'The Conspirators', for instance, presents the commonly advanced distinction between the Christ of the Gospels and the Christ of St Paul in all its misleading weakness. And it is often the firm command of a difficult verse that renders, not palatable but accessible, dogmas advanced in their most naked shape as in 'The Jealous One'. It is that particular 'wrestling with words and meanings' to use Eliot's phrase that is at the heart of much of this work. As Clemo puts it in 'The Awakening':

> For I have much to tell,
> But cannot find the simple word
> By which the common heart is stirred
> Because of this poetic swell
> This fume of fashioning, this need
> To find fit rhythm and tone and there aesthetically feed.

The stirring of the 'common heart' lies close to the practice widespread, at least in former times, in Methodism of the giving of a 'Testimony' – the account of how God has dealt with an individual. The giving of a testimony runs right through Clemo's work. The ways of God which Clemo recounts are strange, often harsh, but powerful and clear. They are nowhere clearer than in 'The Bequest'. This poem has a singular history. Only to be found in the Wheal Martyn archive its manuscript is in the Lockwood Memorial Library of the University of Buffalo. How it came there is not clear, and it has not been traced in published form. Speaking as it does of the influence on him of American evangelists it would seem appropriate that the manuscript should be held in the USA. It is, however, of even broader significance. Its underlying theme is the process of Clemo's deliverance from an environment and personal circumstances which would have been crippling and constricting. At the heart of this, in addition to Clemo's own remarkable tenacity and vision, are the intellectual and spiritual influences which he embraced. That of T.F. Powys has already been mentioned. It found expression at the time of writing of these poems in the poem 'A Kindred Battlefield', to be found in 'The Wintry Priesthood' section of *The Map of Clay,* and later in 'Mappowder Revisited'.[30] 'The Wintry Priesthood' marks other influences as diverse as the great Swiss Protestant theologian Karl Barth, the Danish philosopher and theologian Søren Kierkegaard, D. H. Lawrence – a kindred spirit, though later rejected – and C. H. Spurgeon. It was to the bracing Calvinist teaching of Spurgeon that Clemo turned while still quite a young man. The hitherto unpublished short poem on Spurgeon included here evokes more briefly than the poem in 'The Wintry Priesthood' the courageous isolation of Spurgeon from the climate of his age.[31] Spurgeon's influence in helping deliver Clemo from the 'clay-land winter' in which his brain lies cannot be underestimated.[32] Here too, is a major poem on another – perhaps the greatest – influence on Clemo, that of Robert Browning. For Clemo, the Browning story of a marriage achieved against all human probability was the emblem of how he felt God would deal with him, leading him to marriage against all the constrictions of his human situation, and so it was, as 'flesh is called to share the wondering spirit's search'.

The writing of these poems is part of that process of deliverance and 'awakening' which lies at the heart of Clemo's work and experience. Along with it goes that process of recognition, after many years of obscure struggle, which he found with the publication in the late 1940s and early 1950s of *Wilding Graft, Confession of a Rebel* and of 'The Wintry Priesthood' in the *Poems 1951* Festival of Britain anthology. Clemo was then a poet recognised nationally by figures as distinguished as C. Day Lewis, but equally in his own territory of Cornwall. That recognition was eloquently expressed by his friend and contemporary Charles Causley:

In the deep wood dwells a demon
   Taller than any tree –
His prison bars are the sailing stars,
   His jailer is the sea.

With a brain and ten fingers
   He ties Cornwall to the table
Imagination, at battle station,
   Guards Pegasus in his stable.

He walks the white hills of Egypt
   Reading the map of clay –
And through his night there moves the light
   Artillery of day.

Turn, Cornwall, turn and tear him!
   Stamp him in the sod!
He will not fear your cry so clear –
   Only the cry of God.[33]

That cry of God is awakened here in these newly found poems.

John Hurst
Alan M. Kent

Notes

1. Evelyn Clemo (n.d.) *I Proved Thee at the Waters*, Ilkeston: Moorley's Bible and Bookshop.
2. Letter to Andrew C. Symons, 4/10/87.
3. Jack Clemo (1949) *Confession of a Rebel*, London: Chatto & Windus, pp.61–5.
4. See Jack Clemo (1983) *The Bouncing Hills*, Redruth: Dyllansow Truran.
5. Charles Thomas (1993) *Tintagel: Arthur and Archaeology*, London: Batsford and English Heritage; Amy Hale, Alan M. Kent and Tim Saunders (2000) *Inside Merlin's Cave: A Cornish Arthurian Reader 1000–2000*, London: Francis Boutle, Charles Thomas (1994) *And Shall These Mute Stones Speak? Post Roman Inscriptions in Western Britain*, Cardiff: University of Wales Press, pp.279–80.
6. Conversation with Andrew C . Symons 7/8/75.
7. Jack Clemo (1961) *The Map of Clay*, London: Methuen.
8. Jack Clemo (1948) *Wilding Graft*, London: Chatto & Windus.
9. Jack Clemo (1986) *The Shadowed Bed*, Tring: Lion.
10. Jack Clemo (2000) *The Clay Kiln*, St Austell: Cornish Hillside Publications.
11. Jack Clemo (1972 [1958]) *The Invading Gospel: A Return to Faith*, London: Lakeland, p.52.
12. Ibid., p.38.
13. Ibid., pp. 48–9. Compare with J.C. Trewin and H.J. Willmott (1950) *London-Bodmin*, London: Westaway, pp.89–92.
14. Clemo (1961) op.cit..
15. Letter to Alan M. Kent, 8/5/94. Clemo describes the volume as 'odd in subject'; these poems being 'as non-Cornish as Murano'.
16. Conversation with Evelyn Clemo, 1976.
17. Jack Clemo (1971) *The Echoing Tip*, London: Methuen, (1975) *Broad Autumn*, London: Methuen.
18. Letters to Andrew C. Symons, 12/10/84 and 22/6/85.
19. Letters to Andrew C. Symons, 26/7/89 and 11/12/89.
20. Bede Griffiths (1976) *Return to the Centre*, London: Collins, pp.62–66.
21. Letter to Andrew C. Symons, 11/6/99.
22. Letter to Andrew C. Symons, 18/11/93.
23. See Jack Clemo (1993) *Approach to Murano*, Newcastle upon Tyne: Bloodaxe Books, (1995) *The Cured Arno*, Newcastle upon Tyne: Bloodaxe Books.
24. Ibid., 18/11/93; Letter to Andrew C.Symons, 19/8/93.
25. Jack Clemo (1989) *Banner Poems*, Gorran: Cornish Nationalist Party Publications.
26. Letter to Andrew C. Symons, 11/6/99.
27. Jack Clemo (1951) *The Clay Verge*, London: Chatto & Windus.
28. Clemo (1980) op.cit., pp.65–6.
29. Clemo (1949) op.cit., p.197.
30. Jack Clemo (1986) *A Different Drummer,* Padstow: Tabb House, p.62.
31. It should be acknowledged that Spurgeon was an enormously successful preacher with a warm appreciation of literature and the natural world.
32. 'Cornish Anchorite' is found in 'The Wintry Priesthood' section of *The Map of Clay*. The poem 'Surrender' in the current collection is an earlier version of this poem. Comparison of the two reveals the scrupulous care Clemo brought to the development of his poems.
33. Charles Causley (1975) *Collected Poems 1951–1975*, London: Macmillan, p.50. The reference to Egypt is to a small hamlet near to Clemo's Goonamarris house.

The Poems

Revelations in the Clay Pit

Who needs forgiveness now?
For You had prisoned me
within the walls of pain-dark mystery
And left her free to vow
Her life to other ends and so escape
These damps you chose for me, this mould and grime
which fashions me for monkhood, not the slime
In honest daylight of the hungering clay
That was her choice and somebody must pay.
Why should it not be You
who tore our fates apart and broke the shape
And pattern of the dual stress
Matching the mightiness
Of that articulation I deemed true,
That Word which braves all prisons, bids rejoice.
You would not hear my voice,
And how could I hear Yours
when you were slamming, slamming all my doors?
You spurned my inner light,
And how could I reveal
such rays as faith afforded of the bright
Christ-essence when your hand
was resolute to seal
The windows of my tower through which I scanned
The vain horizons for a trace
Of her returning form? There was no place
For common measurements of sin;
And why did you begin
This wasteful loss of Your own self in me?
Why foolishly redeem?
If with redemption comes the shattered dream
Of human joys which she
Gains without prayer or vision? Why elate
Upon that Easter turret of your power
When I am buried still in His dark hour
And her heaven mocks us both? You know this state

Of infinite wreckage sprung
From trustful heart and glad obedient tongue.
When in the courtyard the world's hammers rang
  Driving the nails for greed
  Of faithless fleshy meed
  And coarsest earthly tang,
I was apart with her and for relief
of that sore martyrdom, even though belief
Flamed in our kisses, not in altar smoke,
  And these dark corridors awoke
To other genuflections than are used
  In churches where His truth is bruised
  By scholarship or art.
  You set us there to start
The blood's crusade against all doubt of Him;
  And yet maliciously
Barred off her blood from faith which grew to me
More beautiful than her own body till
she felt His breath in mine, and then the dim
sick transformation crept through nerves and will,
  And my long destined night
  Closed, following her flight:
  And Your almighty ban
  Forestalled my every plan
  To reach her heaven or His.
  With tasteless ironies
You fill my days for me, this only life
which has no choice but has surrendered all
  In trust that through the strife
  By which I died in Him the Fall
  Would cease to live in her.
  What grace do you confer
Through tricks like these? What love could shape such doom?

These are my facts. What shall my verdict be,
Baptized into such sonship, when this gloom
Breaks at Christ's Judgment seat which sets me free?

Sabbath

Tired villagers crave ease from care
   As church bells stutter o'er the moors
   On neutral air.
They go to stir the winds of prayer
   where they are wont
   In pew and font
To rustle news of Him the Church adores.

I went to her, amid the sleek
   Cool screen of clay-dunes we shall find
   All that they seek.
Our limbs and eyes shall scale the peak
   where God in flesh
   stoops to enmesh
soiled clay with nerve-taps from His upper wind.

Vision of Bethlehem

You and I, beloved, had sought in our human strength
    Vainly for love with its naked soul aflame
With meaning for earth sprung lives; we saw at length
A star in the sky; and following we came
    To a stable in far, old, humble Bethlehem.

We paused on the threshold, wondering at the sight:
    A lantern burning, oxen standing by
with strange hushed breathing; and the silent night
Pierced only by a piteous human cry,
    A sob long drawn, a stifled travail cry.

Midnight of the Soul

That flame in my soul, a pure
　　Golden Robe for God's form,
I felt it would endure
　　Against every storm.
I sang of its broadening, certain,
　　For its glow was fed
By a Christ-pulse thro' blood's curtain
　　where sin is shed.

I never believed that swift stream
　　That burned my thought,
Could be, as a cold sly day-dream,
　　To a standstill brought;
That a word Heaven's link could sever,
　　Clang back the dross.
Mine be the pain forever,
　　God's the loss.

The Burial, Good Friday 1934

Only the shadow now, the shadow of One who died,
   Over my life's day reels that pitiless noon.
The revel of Death for humanity's last hope crushed
   I feel in my brain, for they – oh God, they have lied
When they said He rose, and the millions who have rushed
   To the faith He pillared were duped, and I – so soon.

Death knows Him its captive still, there is no release for man
   Till grave-mould answers the God who failed to care
what poison he sipped, or pity him, blinded, gored
   Into the dark. Death's eager footsteps ran
Glibly to meet Him, knowing His plan to share
   wine of His veins, ripe blood which the Fall ignored.

With reverent, fumbling feet I steal to the tomb
   And drop in the dust my empty goblets, carved
Thro' my faith in Him: there let them mouldering lie.
   And all of my manhood's worth that caught the bloom
Of His imaged vineyard, doomed to be parched and starved,
   Shall wither with Him beneath God's drunken sky.

Cornish Night

Here the sandhills' white on the downs are rearing
   And the ripped pits gape at the sky
with the feeble lights from the lanterns flaring
   where the workmen toil; and the cry
Of some night bird wheeling above them heightens
   The pulse of a terror that glides
Thro' a dark which no streak of dawn glow brightens.

Here the cottages cower in the gloom-girt valley,
   Silent and stark; creep like ghosts
past each shuttered window; cold shapes that dally
   And linger and slink – the hosts
Of dread things abroad in the blackness thickening
   On the hillsides where in fright
A phantom wind in a demon-quickening
   Screams in the womb of night.

Midnight of the Flesh

To lie awake and stretch tired, yearning arms
    where you, girl-phantom of my prison, glide,
And try and make love's wanton, secret charms
    Turn shade to flesh for seed unsatisfied.

To call your name and woo the heedless air,
    To speak, myself, what your ripe voice should say,
And burrow to the craven help of prayer,
    Imploring Him who sneers in this delay.

Is He afraid earth-sparks would foul His lip
    In that great hour when we together cling
As I ascend the fountain steps to dip
    My torch in waters whence the rainbows spring?

Torch that now sears my vitals; Nature still
    Glares with the greedy glint of lecherous fire.
Your breasts are rounded into Calvary's hill,
    And 'gainst the sky His Cross is on the pyre.

Faith in the Empty Garner

Lord, I can bring no sheaves,
  No fruit to swell Thy store;
The year's last star-shaft leaves
  Harsh glint on a barren floor.

Long I have gone forth, far,
  Sowing, and wept in prayer;
Fallen, and glimpsed Thy star,
  Praised when my faith could dare.

Thou in Thy word hast said,
  "Surely he comes again,
Bringing his sheaves." O dead
  Earth, with my sin its bane!

Cleanse while I love Thy clasp
  Hands which have scattered seed,
Precious, then stooped to grasp,
  Fevered, the tempter's weed.

So may I bring, not late,
  sheaves from my worthy field,
Rejoicing that longest wait
  Obtains the richest yield.

Clay Scene in Winter

Upon the downs at evening gorse fires rise,
    A chain of flickering flame thro' smoke that breaks
And rolls in eddies; children's high shrill cries
    Are borne from round these fires, and echo wakes.

Dun rivers roar more sullen; every sound
    Strikes strange and sharp upon the stillness; frost
Lies on earth's rigid face; the frozen ground
    Gives echo of tired feet, and far view's lost.

The sand dunes stand forlorn and grim, and grey
    Now that the snows have melted, purer white
Than sand – Among the deep pits children play,
    Climb, pause at times to watch a lone bird's flight.

During a Thunderstorm

O gloom and wild thunder
That, one with my nature,
I revelled in – tempest,
Combated, depriving,
With strength given for striving,
Your fury of plunder:
Rude battle-force, wager
Of conflict for gain – lest
without Your sure testing my soul, quest resigning,
Seeks ease in false comfort of song and sun shining,
Leave with me Your spirit, life's purpose enshrining?

Perranporth, August 15th, 1934

These great cliffs,
  Turf crowned where rude paths thread,
Kissed by strong breeze and lingering humans' tread
Crannied and torn – here loveliness unspoilt
  Is linked with dread.

These strange seas
  That laugh and fret and squeal,
waves fire capped where the white gulls wheel,
I see, shall know – recapture in kind dream
  Their throbbed appeal.

This wide sweep,
  Of golden, wave-tracked sands,
Firm paradise for children's feet and hands,
Crossed by the lazy stream – is ever held
  In memory's bands.

These vast rocks,
  Aloof grim sentinels,
sea-battered when the in-tide wells –
Arched, twisted, beauty wild and weird –
  Here love-thought dwells.

Goonamarris

Brood of sand-heaps swelling noisy, white and high
      To the sky;
Cottages that flank the splintered pit below
      In a row.
Lonely lane that from the valley steeply climbs,
      Many times
Fidgeting to left and right where under trees
      Nettles tease.

Coppice threading bold and dark-veined, thin beneath
      Earth-scabbed heath;
Fields lean-bellied, straggling, pierced and broken where
      Clay tanks glare.
Beacon domed across the valley, sure to keep
      while I sleep,
world that shatters peace with clamour, curse and shout,
      All shut out.

And when surly visaged winter comes to stay
      Cornwall way,
Grim and stubborn 'neath its savagery here stands,
      Swept by sands
Hamlet braving thunders of the midnight gale,
      Snow and hail –
Mean and patient, clay-splashed birthplace of my moods'
      solitudes.

The Token

A shift of His mood brings an hour's relief
   From His cloudy pressure of grinding grief –
The hammering grief that kills all worth
   Desire for woman, and gifts of earth.

No woman again, no flesh mature,
   With the serpent rhythm in its tidal lure;
But He drops amid my hermit pain
   The old thrill purged of creative stain.

In a field on which the sand-dump spilt
   A vomit of gravel where grasses wilt,
My ice-world broke for an hour of flame
   With one who shared it in childish game.

We romped in the sun, but the warmth I felt
   Came only from her as she tried to pelt
My face into smile with orange peel.
   She skinned the fruit with her teeth – would steal

Close up, undeterred by the threatened smack,
   Her hand clenched tightly behind her back,
Her hand curled warm on the missiles broken,
   Growing soft and moist with her blood's shy token.

She would pull and push till my face was free,
   Then snuggle closer and shower on me
Those silly tokens of childish freak,
   Splintered from Nature – as God might wreak.

Rage on idolators yet in play
   Give their sacred relics as toys away
Mystic imaginings men must shun
   To escape His wrath and share His fun.

No symbol here to adjust, adapt,
　　Be fogged and bogged by: beauty lapped
So calm her childhood's nakedness,
　　I needed not mask its frank caress.

How she would laugh, blessed heretic,
　　If I said this peel so sour and thick
that to my enlightened vision meant
　　The bread of a wondrous sacrament.

I talked so once, embraced the cheat,
　　But the rout of it surely is complete
Now ideals and fancies of every kind
　　Are bitterer than this orange rind.

She is the real: I taste and see
　　Her girlish magic unflinchingly.
Unstripped to Nature's evil core,
　　She shows her bounty of sense the more.

Each scrap of yellow peel she flung
　　Lay fierily on the turf, a tongue
Speaking of bliss I dared not name
　　Till I saw in her the new way it came.

With hints like this I can bear His shade,
　　Nor fear His jealousy's blasting blade,
Back under the cloud: here His eye shall see
　　I am purged at last of idolatry.

Shall I praise Him again when, as Nature's foe,
　　I emerge to deride its creative flow,
Hating flesh and flower when ripe for seed
　　But for sex, bare rind, feeling love indeed?

Clay Fairy

How good to have you here! This dense
   Cold drizzle cannot blur the sense
That clay work and enchanted lies
   Under the witchery of your eyes.

If this fog lifted we should see
   The clay-dunes towering massively
Beyond the pit – a score at least
   Ridging the upland to the east.

A year ago I used to creep
   Each evening to this fence and keep
Tryst with old Death: no muted shape
   But told me I could not escape.

As far as eye could reach the scarred
   Grim landscape stretched, one huge graveyard.
The sand-dumps all like headstones loomed;
   The pits my rotted youth entombed.

The furnace fires where stacks upreared
   Like grisly crematoria glared;
Even the rows of pulley frames
   were crosses over my battle-shames.

But now – what is this sorcery
   That makes a new earth guilelessly?
The hues of your child heart have run,
   Bewitched these objects – every one.

The dumps are fairy castles now
   Which you have climbed with me; they glow
With dancing warmth your footsteps leave;
   The dazzling palpitations heave.

Renunciation

I ask no comfort of mankind,
　　Caress of earth or heaven,
No pang of soul, no grace of mind
　　By beauty given.

Grant but the fulness of one word,
　　And strength to bear the stigma –
The sweetest word in language, Lord:
　　Not 'Love' but 'Dogma'.

A Modern Christian

Priests vie with workmen, heaving Mammon's wall
    Against His terrors: banners of the crowd
United in escape from Him, forestall
    His cross, stream floodlit, fearless, free and proud.

I take my place apart and choose to stare
    At witless clay by lantern light until
My life grows blank of human pride or care,
    Ripened by truths that mould Golgotha still.

When I caught echoes of the workmen's song
    I prayed for idleness; and when priests' hands
Fell in glib blessing on the noisy throng
    I craved a silence where no altar stands.

And yet I worship: not as poets trace
    God's breath in Nature's visionary flame.
Each flower is wan to me as Pilate's face,
    And woodlands share the cities' reeking shame.

It is not peace I seek: the beautiful
    Is meaningless as classic wisdom's lore.
Only His terrors find me dutiful,
    Burning me bare to Incarnation's core.

I feel this secret malice of belief
    Break on their charity as Christ on Hell.
Their falsehoods pass: my death, like His, is brief,
    And followed by the life no lie can quell.

Better be crazed with isolating fear
    Than sane in Brotherhood's pale unity:
Stronger than team work is the lonely tear –
    Greater than fellowship is agony.

The Cursed Tree

Bare it stands, the old Earth-tree,
   Neither Woman nor God to me.
No symbol or message there
   To make me grow aware
How God in mercy stooped and clothed her,
   And clothed Himself till Nature loathed her.

At the breath of the waking Son
   I was blinded, quick to shun
That Mother-tree men prize.
   Then looked with Christian eyes
And saw the old Tree stripped for burning –
   One bud redeemed to share my spurning.

The Conspirators

A Claywork is an awkward place
  For those who doubt redemptive grace.
Christ walks there in His Pauline mood,
  And those who think His ethic good
If kept fastidiously apart
  From notions of man's evil heart,
May hear his laughter break with Paul's
  Derisively as ripped earth falls,
Ironic is the Master's way,
  Plotting with Paul amid the clay,
And where the humanists would sight
  A heaven He strikes with dynamite.

That was Paul's method, they admit,
  And thus they labour still to split
His teaching from the Nazarene's.
  They want to find what beauty means,
And blest tranquility of mind
  In which the nerve of life's refined.
They know that common decency
  Proves natural man's divinity,
And ideals of the helping hand
  Convince them that allied they stand
With Christ the original and true
  Unspotted by the Tarsus Jew.

Impregnation

Youth's tide is sluggish; but a sudden fire
   purples the palsied brine thro' which I cleave,
Rejuvenates the sea, burns weeds that weave
   A net of death for her untaught desire.
It bares my vision to the sea-bed mire
   Below us, where there is no God to grieve
Over bleached bones of lovers. Storms bereave
   Young hearts, strange growths entice them if they tire
In this vast sea of passion. Why is ours
   A fate so different? For the heaven is grey
Above us too with tempest, yet it powers
   Dismayed before the sea's red life, which – stay! –
is a blood that fed Golgotha's flowers
   And pulses in the lips I kiss today.

Prayer for Those in Love

Creeds grow cold above
    Passion's reach:
Christ of creeds and love
    Stoop and teach
Passion how to kiss
    Without shame,
Granting faith a bliss
    Flesh may name.

Virgin's fleshly rose
    Bore Thy thorn;
So the dark womb grows,
    Nor forlorn.
Let love's life, as Thine,
    Taste of blood –
Seed our loins resign
    To Thy rood.

Warmth

Waves of the summer heat
    Flood with the urge
    Of the powers which merge
Beauties till life's complete
    And a heaven lies at man's feet.

Wave upon wave but see
    In the proudest flow
    Of this reckless show
All shadowed by what must be
    When the hot tides turn and flee.

Surge of the blood – divine
    At the human tip
    Where our low lives slip,
Blind, into God's confine,
    Halt, and await His sign –

This, men must know to lose?
    That the soul employ
    All the body's joy,
Is a task too great – the use
    Forbidden by ills profuse?

Not so! While sunlight streams
    And the flesh-desire
    Bids the soul aspire
Christ's Passion-blood redeems,
    Grants Eternity to our dreams.

Summer

Slim sand-hills are rearing
    white peaks to heaven's blue;
Around all Earth's bearing
    Fair fruit for man's view:
Birds' songs and flowers nodding, bee's hum and brook's laughter
    Must bid us Adieu.

Voice, came, still birds' trilling!
    Face, smile as my sun!
Hands, yield for flowers' willing
    My cross now play's done.
One kiss and one prayer-word, one tear for love's sowing –
    Life's summer begun.

Redemption

In close embrace and kissing,
    All thrills that blood can know,
There would be nought worth missing
    Did not Thine own blood flow,
Where fleshy seed is lifted
Love's grain from tares is sifted
Only if men are gifted
    with cleansing while They sow.

For those who live God-spurning
    Flesh knows but lustful sway,
Flame-prick mid darkness burning
    Thro' passing brief today.
With Christ is love's Forever,
No kiss is lost, nor ever
For Death's grim power to sever,
    Shall bodies lose their way.

Surrender

Now decomposed in dogma lies my brain,
All faculties that human growth would stain
Dissolved to weedless nescience. Here is soil
No poet pen can scratch, no culture's light despoil.
This womb beyond earth's reach
Teems with no beauties that can teach
My senses mortal joy or mortal pain.
I am exempt at last
In dogmas fold till Nature's rhythms be overpast.
I feel a truth the death of God has sown,
Truth that draws fibre of human knowledge back
To grey agnostic bone,
Breaks down the nerve of natural piety
To its foul core, turns slack
The muscle of bold self sufficiency,
And lets the once proud clay
In dumb humility decay.
There is no worship here, only the worm we call
Original sin, and fire of the Fall.
Worm and fire at my roots, how should I know
Your sunlight, song of your birds, you poet brood?
How should I share your pagan glow
Who hate your flowers, your seasons? Food
For these is in your blood but not in me.
I rot past Nature towards a birth
Of heaven's fertility
That blasphemes spring upon your earth.

Caprice of a Jealous One

The whirlwind heat is past:
Its desolating blast,
    Has killed
   What Nature tilled.

All stains she treasured
Are now to blankness bled.
    She lied,
   And I have died.

To all except the Truth.
Dead to my mortal youth,
    Beyond
   Each trivial bond,

Neither to blood nor soil
Can I henceforth be loyal;
    Among men
   No citizen.

'Tis not for unity
I stand, but mutiny –
    For war
   On bonds that bar.

Faith's old divisions out:
Well may they prize their doubt,
    Snug mood
   Of brotherhood!

Now separate unto Him
I have nought else to limn
    With art
   Of reborn heart.

Yet in His calm's response
There's hint – the same that once
    Brought blame:
    Shall faith reclaim

One spark from Nature's dust,
One that can 'scape the gust
    Of His
    Wild jealousies?

The thaumaturgic change
Thrills all within that range
    Which He
    Deems safe for me.

Perhaps those bounds include
New fleshly rapture – nude
    Desire
    Of saintly fire.

God's is no blind caprice:
And hopes for more than peace
    Convulse
    My waking pulse.

And not by barrenness
Can heavenly mercy bless
    This sore
    Pre-nuptial core.

If I dare soon retrace
My clay-path earthward – place
    My hand
    In His who scanned

Predestinatingly
Each face that I shall see –
    Why, then
    Not as on men

Would smiles and glances light
On my elective sight.
     Nor could
   A mating mood

Strike me until I saw
The one form which His law
     Had signed,
   with me aligned.

So I may feel the sting,
His love whim hardening,
     And gain,
   Beyond the bane,

Beyond my death and hers,
The new earth's joy which spurs
     Our clay
   On heaven's way.

Restoration

So wan with wisdom drifts this age,
And sick with sneers that please the sage:
God's hymn: cut them from rage.

He needs our joys of years long fled,
For feasts eternal. Moments sped
Made precious so, He kneads to bread.

And needing thus, He'll newly pour
Wine we have known if to the core
Our hearts retain their thirst of yore.

So 'mid the thickening clouds and weeds
Here's answer to the fool who feeds
On dust: Sun, flowers we knew, God needs.

The True Optimism

What say New Year bells
    Swift or slow
As they ring, they glow
    Echoes at the clash of heavens and hells.

What says New Year hush
    peaceful birth –
But the vulgar earth
    Loves its noise, will keep its warfare's rush.

This meandering, mild
    welcome dawn
Ere the year be gone
    Shall for all be lost in thunders wild.

Face the worst – invite
    No vain hope,
So the horoscope
    Of earth's evil shall be read aright.

And the stars be seen,
    Stars of God
Mixing for the clod
    Fires that torture that they may make clean.

St Dennis

As sudden as a man beholds his end
   Carne Hill loomed, scarred and grim to consecrate
Topping the vale, and wildly to descend
   The slope to bleakness where the moor fowl prate
Of summer every house seemed minded, crazed
   With sun. And to me came the strange, supreme,
Unheard-of wonder – that amid the mazed
   Muddle of house roofs garish to redeem
The encircling savagery, there day by day
   God holds perpetual Sabbath. Laggard twine
The lowland cottage smoke-tufts; they would stay
   And float as incense round one human shrine.

Autumn Dawn

Along the tattered ridge of night
  Swift needles quiver, dazzling bright,
Gather the strips of cloud which droop
  Forlornly o'er the hills, and loop
  Each grey patch with a thread of light.

The sun's hand knows no pause or hitch;
  On fiery needles, stitch by stitch,
It weaves the vestment of new day.
  Dawn shadows reel, as though they stray
  Near tomb or birth-bed, doubting which.

The world is silent, scarce a breeze
  Profanes the mute chill grieving trees.
A ragged sleeve of cloud I trace
  That flaps a sand-dump's sombre face
  Above the valley's huddled frieze.

The fierce red needles halt. Up rears
  The burning hand on sun. Earth wears
Her living robes, sun-woven for
  Its coming as her paramour,
  And light-embraced, forgets her cares.

Inspiration

Oh, for the agony – sweet wild sting of the hour!
   Prostrate the mind as the spirit strains into birth;
Boring of words to burst from their pressing tower,
   Unsullied and free from the virginal taint of dearth.

Barren the poet's brain if his flesh be loathed;
   Naked he stands, entreating you, cold on the heights.
No fires can he wrest from God, nor will he be clothed
   Till, quickened by you, he knows how the earth requites.

Come to that mind, O seed in a girl's eyes hidden,
   Lie and be lured to the silence that love enjoins;
Mystery of inspiration, unfold as bidden
   Hues that soak in the shadow of pressing loins.

Come to that mind, oh seed which a girl's eyes chasten;
   Barren the womb where a new star should be grown,
Needing a pulse from immortal lips – oh hasten!
   Pining in darkness for want of a life unknown.

Towards the Dawn

Joy shall stream in morning light
  When this hour of dark be done,
Fiercest conflict of the night
  Issue in glad victories won:
  Of these shadows vain are none:
    By God's might
  Each shall fade in endless sun.

Conscious of thy erring ways
  Thou art stricken with regret;
Still, dishonouring God's days
  Oft come moods of doubt and fret,
  And thy heart is troubled – yet
    Shall God's praise
  Flood where thy life's goal is set.

Climbing, weary of thy cares,
  Let not aspiration tire,
Lured at times by Satan's snares
  From God's path to perils dire
  Know that God, thro' storm and briar
    Hears thy prayers,
  Holds thee, guards, leads ever higher.

Tho' thine aim be often marred
  By the stain of selfish thought,
Yet shall God in cleansing guard
  Each desire which Thou hast brought
  Humbly to His service – nought
    Shall be barred,
  But be blessed while Thou art taught.

A Hymn of Praise

From Heaven Thou camest, stooping low
   To bear the fruit of mortal toil,
   And in the baseness of our soil
Rooted the life which knows no woe!

In Thee alone is joy complete,
   Tho' oft obscuring questions crowd,
   And staggered at distress allowed,
Faith owns its weakness at Thy feet.

Thou only, Christ, art One apart,
   We know not loneliness like Thine;
   Our sorrows lack the touch Divine
Until they centre in Thine heart.

Thou only, God and man, art true;
   Thy love alone unfaltering speeds;
   Thy power, adapting to our needs,
Stilleth the whirlwind, spreads the dew.

From Thee, incarnate God, there spring
   Joys of the morn when loves aspire;
   And when life's stifling noontides tire
Thy cleansing breath supports our wing.

Thy Blood alone, O God, shall warm
   The slopes where death in mockery waits;
   The fire of human blood abates,
Chilled by the hurrying night's alarm.

No name but Thine, O Christ, shall glow
   Upon the shields of Christian strife;
   The treasured trophies of our life
Are shattered else before the foe!

For mercies shown accept our praise,
    The praise of hearts too stubborn long.
    Till thrilling with Thy love our song
Is fit to testify Thy ways!

Unclothed

I have waited through the ages
    For this one hour of time
When I should take a body
    And challenge the world's crime.

For I have caught grave secrets
    From the laughter of paradise;
The healing of man's sorrows
    Is spread before my eyes.

My voice would stir the nations
    With strong zeal to prefer
Peace, love, and these establish,
    If clothed in flesh I were.

On earth are a man and woman,
    Married unhappily,
For they are the chosen couple
    God meant should ask for me.

Yes, this is God's appointment,
    That they, to end despair,
Should clothe me with their passion,
    And ask for me with prayer.

Instead they ask for pleasure
    (Oh, long shall be their night,
And darker and darker grow the world,
    Denied by saving light.)

They spend their marriage blessing
    In blood that cannot mate;
I think they call it birth-control,
    But it fills God's soul with hate.

The chance is lost: that couple
   To death their race condemn.
I'm ever alone in heaven,
   But Hell is agape for them.

The Divine Lover

No human tongue should stutter
In doubt, but sing for pride
That God of dust has fashioned
A girl to be His bride.

Men should not seek in misery
The dark root of their wars.
But clasp the healing secret
Flung from the Christmas stars.

Mid all the world's strange sorrow
I know a strange relief:
That God has kissed Our Lady
And Their son has kissed our grief.

Prototype

The blood that drips down from His cross
    Shall touch the human seed.
Press closer, love; our founts engross
    His thought, and not our creed.

All lost to love in that great Break
    When Eden woke to shame
He has restored; come, let us take
    Fire at His fleshly flame.

Here where earth rends, and in the gloom
    The pale-domed Temple cowers,
Another garden fair shall bloom
    Beneath your whiter towers.

A future dusk shall gentler brood
    Where on the stripped wood He
Braves Jewry's sky; in less dread mood
    The birth-blood stains your tree.

Immortality

There is one sin against religion's dust
   That makes the wide world sinless with new trust:
To know, tho' churches be but sepulchres,
   One temple with the Cross abhorred of lust.

This He had raised to His own Image height,
   Who with His hair, hath mantled beauties white,
Who with His eyes hath burned one idol more
   Where there are lips whose kisses He may write.

This blasphemy diviner than new creed,
   Old as the urge of Eden's nuptial need,
Shall rise when tome and temple fall dismayed,
   And chant the immortal deity of seed.

The Reporter

Ten thousand dead, the war reporters feared,
   Housed at the Front – when a colleague appeared.
Notebook in hand, he came in thro' the mud:
   He could not write – his hand was streaming blood.
"A bullet thro' the hand, sir – better go – – –"
   The stranger shook his head, smiled wanly – "No;
I only feel the nails again," said He,
   "I felt – do you remember? – on the Tree."

In packed cathedral aisles the preacher's voice
   Gave some reporters reason to rejoice.
"His teachings, heed, digest them, wisdom's feast;
   As for the myth, the Cross – – –" The preacher ceased,
Aghast to see one, notebook still unused,
   And face so sudden white, bloodstained and bruised.
"What ails you?" "I but feel again," said He,
   "Thorns that are doubts of Him who died for thee."

The Awakening

Fate meant that I should walk our earth
In derelict disguise,
Shuffling beneath these icy Cornish skies,
Aware of menace from some hidden sea,
The flicker and pulsation, magnetism
Of cold inhuman currents working schism
In the sharp thorn's shadow, sagging fast
Over the silent clay-world dearth,
The scabbed anomaly
On which the ironic stars look down
With baleful frown
To await the last
Convulsions of the smitten heart
When hopeless trust has failed,
Thorn pierced too deep and pull of the tide prevailed.

There is but one escape from Fate's dream-sodden groove;
With its direction all the moods of our existence move
Once we are set apart.
Even genius sinks,
Swallowed within the vortex of its Nature's need
And thrusts to light putridity decreed
By rootless fibres' friction with the tide that slinks
Through every cleft of our mortality.

Within the narrow Pentecost, direct
Appeal and testimony to the Lord's elect.
For I have much to tell,
But cannot find the simple word
By which the common heart is stirred
Because of this poetic swell,
This fume of fashioning, this need
To find fit rhythm and tone and there aesthetically feed.
Men see the poise and colour of my phrase.
But miss the heavenly blaze.

And the true values stand so sure:
The self-fulfilled alone is really poor,
And the most sacred stain
Upon the nullity of spirit brings no gain;
For God will use
Only what men abuse.
The tumbled gaucheries of a platitude
He has imbued
with fertilising force denied to art;
And in the New Creation's paradox the trite
Alone displays His might.
And we, the complex, the original, must bear
The pang of knowing that our share
In His redemptive Plan is least,
Most impotent
Because most rich in alien potency
By very plenitude of sin increased,
In wilful procreation blent
With Nature, breeding human pride
And splendour of the spirit which must now be crucified
In the new Day's reversal of all values, the decree
That every mouth be stopped
While grace invades, abases and destroys,
And with each shoot of mortal skill and wisdom lopped
In total loss,
Christ holds the Sum of joys,
No tree upon our land except his Cross.

The Legend of Blackrock

"Still at your labours, Featherstone?
Your prison of schist, so mournfully jutting
On Widemouth shore looks grim, as if shutting
Its secret safe where its clefts are entwined.
Is your spirit that here is still confined
Restless still as the grey waves plunging,
Working vainly as winds' fierce lunging,
To weave a web of the stubborn sand?"
  "When the hot sun blisters must I weave them,
  'Mid foulest storms I cannot leave them:
  The baffling sands
      Slips as my hands
        Receive them!"

"Why do this penance, Featherstone?
What crime thus chains you to doom so tragic?
Were you a dabbler in Black Magic?
Did you sell your soul, as a Cornish Faust,
To the Evil One, that your peace is lost?
Was it thirst for knowledge, dark, unlawful,
That laid you under a curse so awful?
Or were you merely a common wrecker?"
  "A wrecker I was! For my lights ensnaring,
  For my gain obtained thro' a course unsparing,
  I writhe in stress –
      Now of success
        Despairing!"

"Your torture must surely end, sometime, Featherstone!
This labour, though vain, must certainly hasten
The hour of release – 'tis meant but to chasten ....
What! At your last wreck, close to this shore,
You stood with a cable, while thro' the roar
Of wind and sea, the drowning, in anguish,
Called for your aid, and you let them languish?
Ah! Tis for this that you now are plagued?"

"Yes! And not till my stained dark soul I cover
With sand-robe made where their cries still hover,
Will my ghastly doom,
                    In sun or gloom,
                        Be over!"

Charles Haddon Spurgeon

Between two seas you died:
The blue Mediterranean upon which
Your heavy eyes last brooded; and there, there,
Behind the eyes that other tide,
The spent edge, the twitch
Of clammy ripples from that poisonous flood
That bruised your spirit, sucked your blood
Before it flung you here, outcast,
Prophet unrecognized! The glare
Of hostile faces in far England comes
In sick drifts to the breaking strand
As from a nightmare past,
Fleering to depths no other mortal plumbs
And few would understand.

The Bequest

Part of me, then, had escaped
Before the nightmare stripped disguise
From my treasured symbols. That fancy I shaped
Here in the granite-damps of my room
On a winter's day – the facile jutting
Scratched out, the false threads knotting.
The tangles tossed in creative fume,
Until the clear-cut lines emerged,
Making a poem – I little dreamed
It would lie where now it lies,
Or what fates converged,
While I wrote, around my cosmos of clay.

A trifling gift, a moulded thought,
Lodged in a sunny home, then horror streamed
On my pit-bed: every image caught
Some monstrous plague, and corruption teemed
In the betrayed heart's questionings.

When Cornish sinews crumbled and turned black
To my vision – when native springs
Were gutted and I lay
Parched on the sand – there came a ray
Out of the west, over the broad sea.
It was America, revival-red,
Which sent her signals, healed and nourished me
Till purged of poisoning granite-dyes,
I stood amazed, so brilliant were the skies.
My spirit tingled with heaven's flash
From gay Los Angeles, the quick pulse from Tulsa,
The bright voice where the alligators fed
In sun-drowsed Carolina swamps.

My odyssey is far out,
Now, from the clay-blast, the sickly wash
Down the cliffs of my fate. I stand

Within God's country, sharing the victory shout
Of the crusader: neon-texts of the camps
Swing through my nerves and claim me back
From the grim cave, the fetid sand.

Strange flotsam beached before the storm,
Those scrawls of fancies! My bequest
Sped like a blind appeal to the warm
Land which has answered and given me rest.

Moment of Dubiety

Fantastic Cornish land that freed
My darkness, can it meet my need
Now that the floods of night recede?

Can claywork idiom be mine
In hours when fruitful favours shine,
Call for a faith's authentic sign?

To what end is this refuse piled
Now that the soil I once reviled
Promises harvest undefiled?

How shall the snarl of splintering blast
Interpret a life intact, held fast
Above the shock, beyond the past?

I am tired of Cornwall, tired of clay
Now that I feel the quickening day
Dissolve the nightmare, press the grey

Sick tones of twilight from my soul?
Incongruous now, my spirit's whole
Vision escapes from clay's control.

Land of the night's blunt probing fang,
Of blundering thrust and deafening clang,
Corroded rock and kiln-fire's tang!

In dubiety I raise my head
From these scarred entrails, from the dead
Dull glowering passion of this bed.

Purgation's landscape failed to purge,
And left me with each human urge
Fouled by the fear of slapping surge

From hose-jets, gore of pouncing tool,
Rotted by stagnant water, cruel
Mauling of micas. Dogma's rule

Was here but travestied by coarse
Bleared symbols: the smoke-blunted, hoarse
Clay-voices rasped my creed – its source

Beyond earth and clay I could not scan
While dunes encompassed, earth-shocks ran,
Smoke towered and knotted, laid the ban

Upon my eyes that groped in vain
To see God's sunshine, feel His rain
Fall fresh above the clay-world's stain.

Robert Browning

But Venice answers Vence: clay fell but light arose
With all the radiant hues of sense transfigured – those
Last alien years tell how: the mask above each scar
Where light was buried till the blood released the star
To fuse afresh with star the blood had known, must know
Transformed in full maturing of its earthly glow.

No baffled search was yours; no bristling dubiety
Infested twilit trails, made faith anomaly.
With piercing signals of election all your days
You knew the separate path, the separate pang and praise
For perilous truths made safe where chosen souls who live
To discipline the nerve find nerve grow primitive.

To some the urge is given to find how flesh can be
Soul's equal, yet not sin nor miss eternity.
Faith has some blisses still which striving sex may name,
And in the recognition split the heavenly flame,
Receiving to its earthly bed the meteorite
From planetary orbits of the spirit's flight.

Upon your life the symbols of this mission closed
With guidance adequate: you saw the problem posed
Within the context of its true solution – just
The simple Christian piety that cancels lust,
Faith of the home and chapel – Calvin's stubborn creed
That Pippa turned to song and naught could supersede.

Yet when you first saw Italy your faith had waned
To glimmer without focus; Shelley's flare had stained
The borderline with softly pagan prophecies
Of priapetic quest in groves and altars: these
Had bred revolt and disillusion: senses swoon
In scent and colour but you lack the crucial boon.

The flash through nadiral nerve from the believing soul's
Calm zenith of effulgence: what hid law controls

The upward glances sundering the flame, diverse
In motive, far apart in quest as yours and hers
Who waits you as the hot south splendours fade, retreat,
And leave you in grey fog through which looms Wimpole Street?

Here's Calvin's world again: elected hour and mood,
Converging glances from two hearts whose faith has stood
The diverse testing – yours the worldling's vacuous snare,
And hers the tidal plenitude of grief till prayer
Craves but release of soul from the tormented pulse
Recoiling in the cloister where grim tides convulse.

Yet flesh is called to share the wondering spirit's search;
The double fusion here decreed must risk the smirch
From smouldering elements as core of faith divides,
Pierced by the upward gaze which passion blends and guides.
Your glimmer stirs to blaze of certainty again
Her visionary light burns red from kindled vein.

Then back to Italy with dower no eye can scan,
The mystic sensuous ardour of the Puritan;
Earth's excess nourished in the boundaries of grace,
The wayward meteorite grown precious in its place.
And thus fulfilled within the narrow code and creed,
You prove faith's paradox, the death grows life indeed.

For this is patterned life, the promise and the test,
The vindication and enjoyment, praise and rest;
The life apart as priest of passion, disciplined
By influence from the zenith, plastic stress of wind
That tempered witness when the answering voice was stilled,
Heard by faith only and the faith benumbed and chilled.

To gain the complex resurrection, sharing here
With flesh the burden and the hunger, strife and fear,
But resolute in knowledge that this love had been
Enough for earth as hint of what such longings mean
Beyond the natural use, within the Moment gripped,
Flung beyond Fate to potency when earth is stripped.

Sanctuary

Cerne and Buckfast lay meek
In western rain, ready for retreats,
Offering negative shelter.
I passed the austere abbeys,
Feeling respect, no kinship.

I was venturing back, on holiday,
To Cornish clay-wastes: I had memories
Of a hermit phase there, but unmarked
By trance or laceration
Of ordered meditation, bell or chant.

No monk or lonely pilgrim
Would fathom the brisk hints
That broke the clay barrier,
Brewed for me a honeymoon in Venice!

Back Home

Nearly home from Dorset: we've just stopped
    At the hillside post-office to collect
Sundry arrears. I'm not much tired,
    But there's a jumbled retrospect.

Soon I shall step on the gateless path
    Where the old wall tap has lost its screw,
And past the gruff and chunky shrubs
    I'll carry my luggage, worn or new.

Pause at the door till someone turns
    A key in the three-months-silent lock,
Then I'll try to connect, touch table, desk,
    Bookcases and the unwound clock.

It will take me days to feel I'm back
    In the rooms I howled at from my pram,
And to sense the humped clay-mound outside,
    Where I once shaped verse on a rusty tram.

St Agnes Church

Where once I sought the healing flash
   Beside the bruising sea,
   My wife now shines on me,
And all my world is blithely brash
Where once I sought the healing flash
   Beside the bruising sea.

Where I confessed the priestly skill
   And haggard gulls still wailed,
   A love invades, unstaled;
The once sick heart can take its fill
Where I confessed the priestly skill
   And haggard gulls still wailed.

When in my youth I grazed these pews
   My life was worn and cold,
   But now I'm back and bold
With bubbly truths I feared to choose
When in my youth I grazed these pews
   And earth seemed worn and cold.

Hensafraen

Hensafraen, the farmyard gate,
And still only half-way down
To the crook of Rosevallon. I recall the steep dip
From the humped block of clay-tanks
And the cowering smear of the cottage
We had just left furtively – not my home.

The broad pathless face dropped headlong
To the infant Fal, a smothered stream
Fighting off silt from Meledor.
We sought peace, swinging the gate open,
Watched by an arrogant rash of cones
On the converging hill.

Our goal was the farmhouse:
We were fetching milk in the lunch-hour
Break from school, and we seemed
The only bearers of young life,
Stretching hands blindly through a sour summer.

Further reading

The Major Works of Jack Clemo:
Wilding Graft, London: Chatto & Windus, 1948
Confession of a Rebel, London: Chatto & Windus, 1949
The Clay Verge, London: Chatto & Windus, 1951
Poems 1951, Harmondsworth: Penguin, 1951★
The Invading Gospel, London: Geoffrey Bles, 1958
The Map of Clay, London: Methuen, 1961
Penguin Modern Poets 6, Harmondsworth: Penguin, 1964★
Cactus on Carmel, London: Methuen, 1967
The Echoing Tip, London: Methuen, 1971
Broad Autumn, London: Methuen, 1975
The Marriage of a Rebel, London: Gollancz, 1980
The Bouncing Hills, Redruth: Dyllansow Truran, 1983
A Different Drummer, Padstow: Tabb House, 1986
The Shadowed Bed, Tring: Lion, 1986
Selected Poems, Newcastle upon Tyne: Bloodaxe Books, 1988
Banner Poems, Gorran: CNP Publications, 1989
Clay Cuts, Church Hanborough: Previous Parrot Press, 1991
Approach to Murano, Newcastle upon Tyne: Bloodaxe Books, 1993
The Cured Arno, Newcastle upon Tyne: Bloodaxe Books, 1995
The Clay Kiln, St. Austell: Cornish Hillside Publications, 2000
★ *Clemo is included in the selection.*

A Selection of Critical Studies:
Davie, Donald, 'A Calvinist in Politics: Jack Clemo's "Confession
    of a Rebel" ' in *Poetry Nation Review*, Vol.6, No.1, 1979
Hurst, John, 'Literature in Cornwall' in Payton, Philip (ed.),
    *Cornwall Since the War: The Contemporary History of a European
    Region*, Redruth: Institute of Cornish Studies and Dyllansow
    Truran, 1993

'Voice from a White Silence: The Manuscripts of Jack Clemo' in Payton, Philip (ed.), *Cornish Studies: Three*, Exeter: University of Exeter Press, 1995

Hutchings, Monica, 'The Cornish Rebel' in *West Country Magazine*, Summer, 1951

Jones, H.L. 'Clay Prophet' in *New Beacon*, Dec. 1960

Isaac, Peter, *A History of Evangelical Christianity in Cornwall*, Cornwall: Peter Isaac, 2000

Kent, Alan M., 'The Cornish Alps: resisting romance in the clay country' in Westland, Ella (ed.), *Cornwall: The Cultural Construction of Place*, Penzance: The Patten Press and the Institute of Cornish Studies, 1997
The Literature of Cornwall: Continuity, Identity, Difference 1000–2000, Bristol: Redcliffe, 2000
Pulp Methodism: The Lives and Literature of Silas, Joseph and Salome Hocking, St. Austell: Cornish Hillside Publications, 2002

Magnusson, Sally, *Clemo: A Love Story*, Tring: Lion, 1986

Martin, E.W., 'The Loneliness of Jack Clemo' in Val Baker, Denys (ed.) *The Cornish Review*, No.5, 1967

Pearce, Brian Louis, *Clemo the Poet: Study and Colloquy*, Twickenham: Magwood, 2002

Press, John, *Rule and Energy*, Oxford: Oxford University Press, 1963

Rowland, John, *One Man's Mind*, London: S.C.M. Press, 1952

Spinks, Michael, 'Jack Clemo: Poet of Sight and Sound' in *An Baner Kernewek/The Cornish Banner*, No.109, 2002

Symons, Andrew C., 'Clemo, Kent and Clay' in *An Baner Kernewek/The Cornish Banner*, No.74, 1993
'Jack Clemo's Italian Holiday' in *Journal of the Royal Institution of Cornwall*, Vol.3, 2000
'Clemo's Clay Inferno' in *An Baner Kernewek/The Cornish Banner*, No.104, 2001

Trewin, J.C. and Willmott, H.J., *London-Bodmin*, London: Westaway Books, 1950

Williams, Derek, 'Writing of Cornwall ... Jack Clemo' in *An Baner Kernewek/The Cornish Banner*, No.59, 1990

Woolsey, Stephen A., 'The Awkward Blessing: Jack Clemo and the Poetic Vision of Grace' in *Mars Hill Review*, No.13, 1999

Other titles from Francis Boutle Publishers

The High Tide: Collected Poems in Cornish 1974–1999
Tim Saunders. ISBN 0953238865 £10 paperback 198 pages
One of the leading poets writing today in the Cornish language. Cast in a
wide range of poetic forms, his work is varied in mood and theme, moving
from the lyrical and intimate to meditations on war and explorations of the
history and culture of Cornwall. Translations into English by the author.

The Wheel: An Anthology of Modern Poetry in Cornish 1850–1980
Edited by Tim Saunders, with a history of the Cornish revival by Amy Hale.
ISBN 0953238873 £10 paperback 224 pages
The first ever survey of poetry in the Cornish language. Represented here
are important figures from the early revival of Cornish, Henry Jenner and
Robert Morton Nance, as well as writers like Tony Snell, Richard Gendall,
Donald Rawe and Saunders himself, who have brought confidence and
maturity to the language. Translations into English by the editor.

**Voices from West Barbary: An Anthology of Anglo-Cornish Poetry
1549–1928**
Edited by Alan M. Kent. ISBN 0953238881 £10 paperback 223 pages
The riches of Anglo-Cornish poetry from the Renaissance to the twentieth
century. Authors include Sidney Godolphin, Humphry Davy, John Harris,
Robert Stephen Hawker (author of *The Song of the Western Men*, better
known as 'Trelawny') and Arthur Quiller Couch, as well as less well-known
figures like Margaret Ann Courtney, James Dryden Hosken and the
anonymous broadsheet writers who helped shape the poetic landscape of
Cornwall.

Looking at the Mermaid: A Reader in Cornish Literature 900–1900
Edited by Alan M. Kent and Tim Saunders ISBN 1903427010 £15
paperback 366 pages. Translations into English by the editors.
Extensive selections from the great works of Cornish literature – the
Ordinalia, Pascon agan Arluth, Beunans Meriasek and *The Creacion of the World* –
with a multitude of poems, letters, proverbs and songs in Cornish, all newly
translated. Dozens of additional texts in English and translation – from
Latin, Anglo-Saxon and French, provide a continuous commentary on the
Cornish language over a millennium.

Inside Merlin's Cave: A Cornish Arthurian Reader 1000–2000
Edited by Alan M. Kent, Amy Hale and Tim Saunders ISBN 1903427045 £12.50
paperback 254 pages
Selections from Geoffrey of Monmouth, Malory's *Morte D'Arthur*,
Tennyson's *Idylls of the King* and A.S.D. Smith's Cornish-language
masterpiece *Trystan hag Ysolt (Tristan and Isolt)*, as well as numerous poems,
prophecies, and plays, including the full text of Thomas Hardy's *Queen of
Cornwall*, reclaim Cornwall as the inspiration of the Arthurian legend.

John Clare and the Folk Tradition
George Deacon ISBN 1903427118 £15 paperback 400 pages
The book contains nearly 300 tunes collected by Clare, as well as numerous
songs and descriptions of the folk customs and beliefs of his native village,
Helpston in Northamptonshire, giving us a unique view into the
disappearing pre-industrial culture of the early nineteenth century.
Deacon's classic work – in paperback for the first time – establishes the
relationship between the folk culture and Clare's development as a poet.

To order any of these titles:

Ring 020 8889 7744 (24hrs)

E-mail info@francisboutle.demon.co.uk

Write to Francis Boutle Publishers
272 Alexandra Park Road, London N22 7BG

www.francisboutle.demon.co.uk